A
Rookie
reader®
TREASURY

Wait, Skates!

and Other

Funny Stories

Children's Press®
An Imprint of Scholastic Inc.
New York • Toronto • London • Auckland • Sydney
Mexico City • New Delhi • Hong Kong
Danbury, Connecticut

Dear Rookie Reader,

What's funny about **skates** or **pickles**?
What's funny about **keeping busy**?
What's funny about **sharing**?
You will find out in this book!

Have fun and keep reading!

P.S. Don't forget to check out
the fun activities on pages 124–127!

Contents

Wait, Skates!

By Mildred D. Johnson
Illustrated by Rick Stromoski

Wait!

The first time on my roller skates,

I tried to make my skates wait.

But they would not wait.

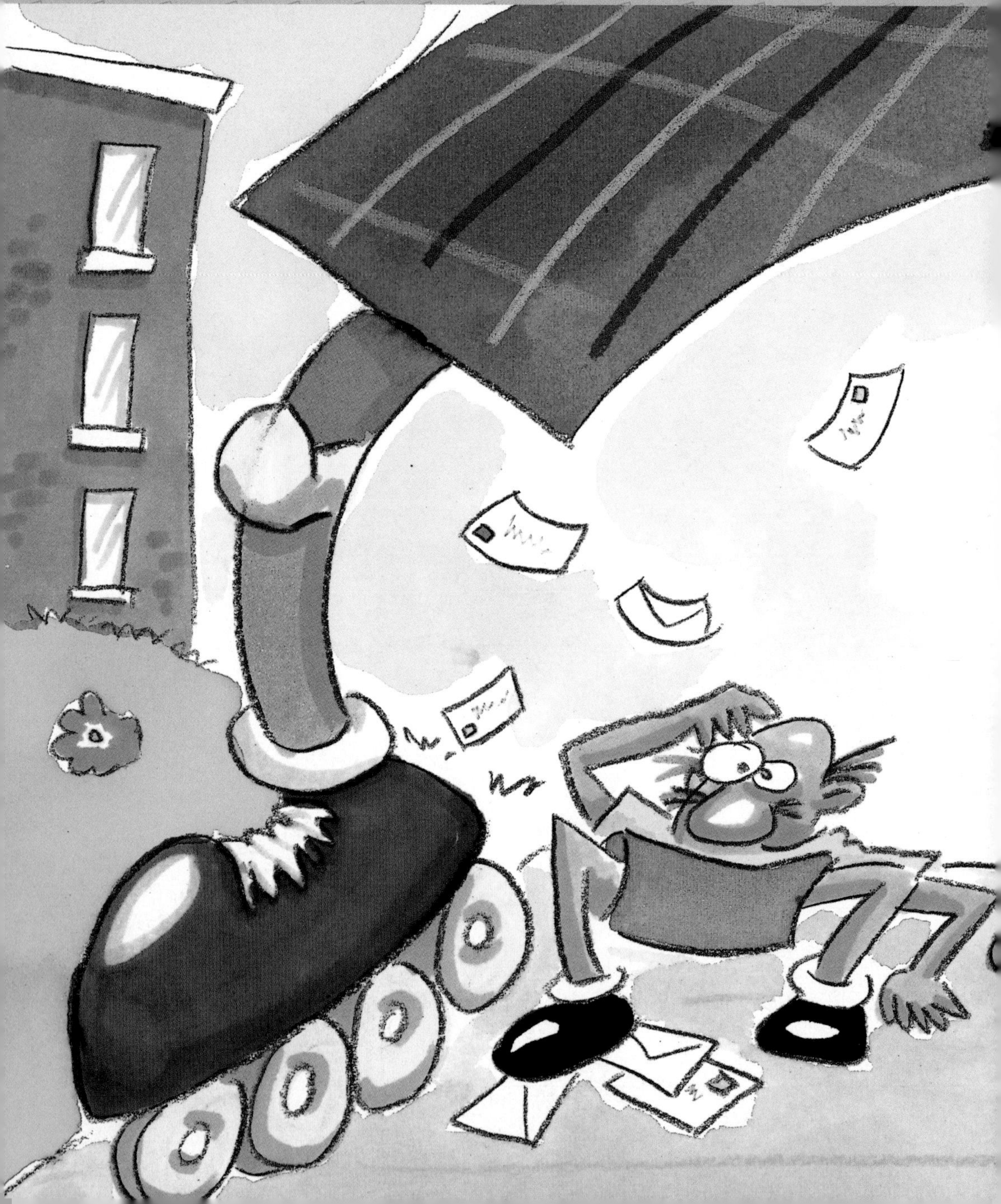

They went out

and sometimes in.

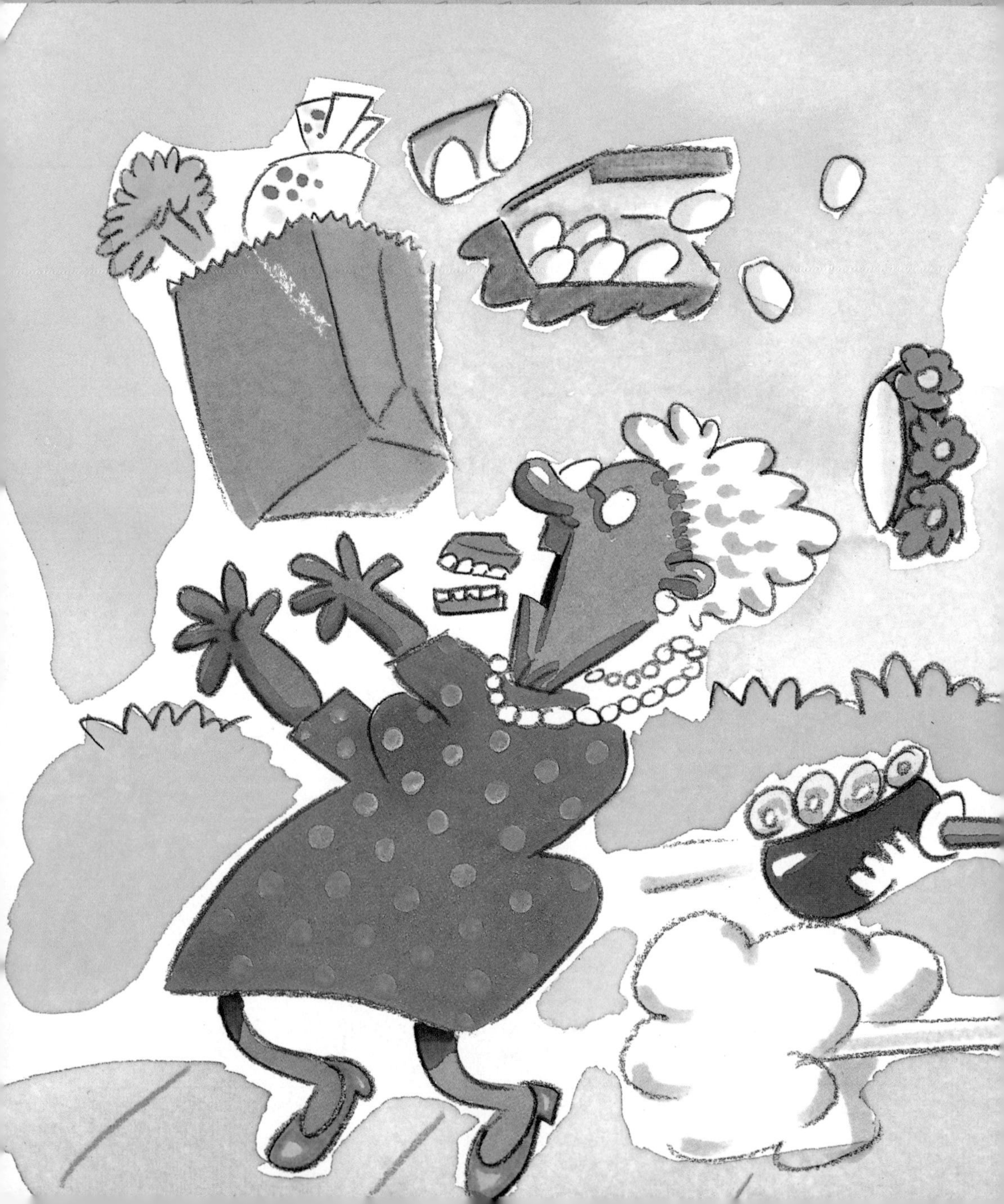

They would not wait.

They would not go straight.

and said out loud . . .

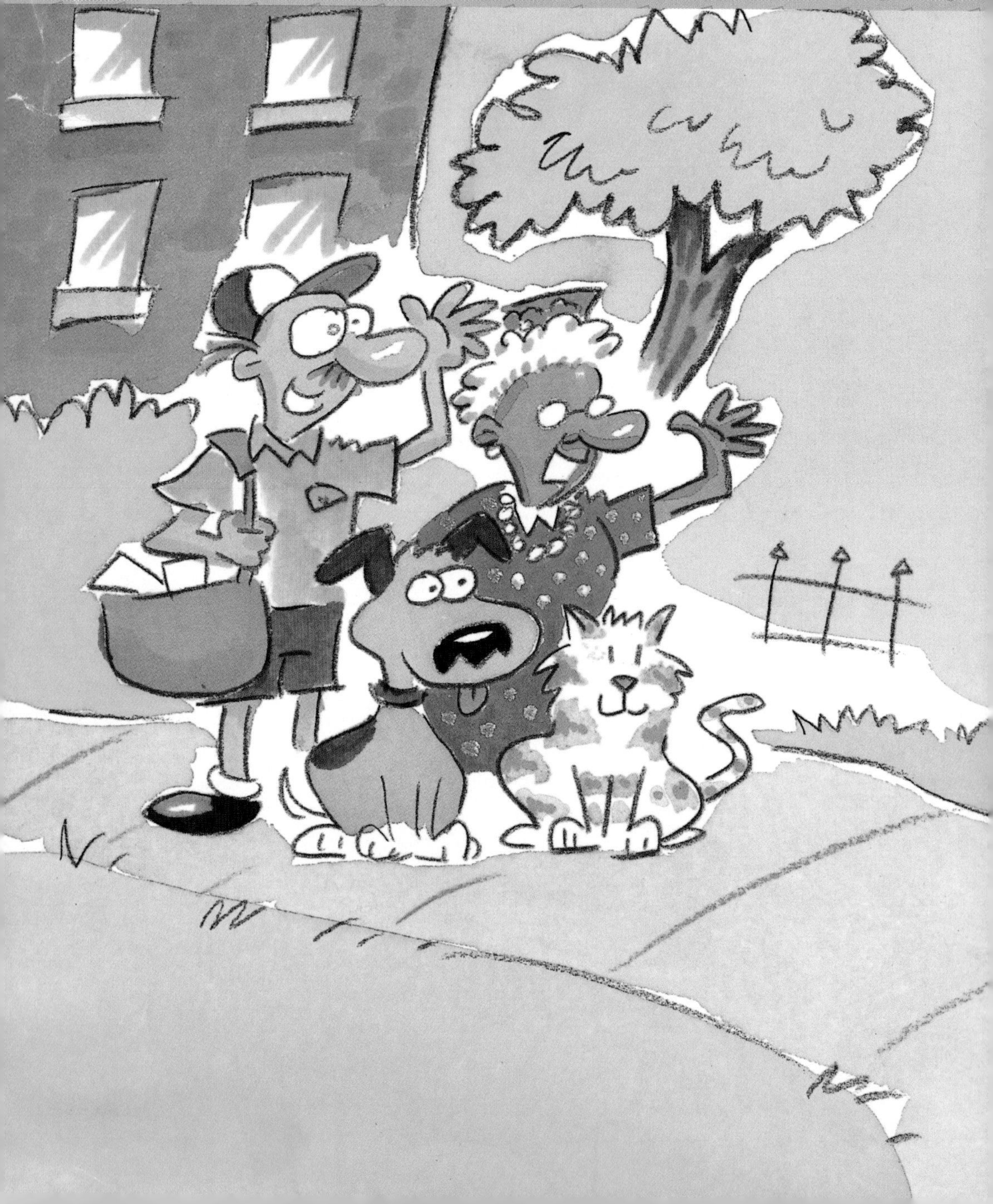

Now I just sail along.

My skates go straight.

Pickles in My Soup

By Mary Pearson

Illustrated by Tom Payne

Pickles! Pickles!
I love pickles.

They are all I want to eat.

I slice them on my cereal.

I slap them on my meat.

Pickles in spaghetti,

pickles all alone,

pickles in my pudding,

and on my ice cream cone.

Pickles topped with onions,

pickles with baloney,

oh, and I really love
pickles in macaroni.

Pickles dipped in chocolate,

pickles rolled in flakes,

pickles on my pizza,

pickles on pancakes!

Pickles in my soup,

pickles on my cake.

Stop! No more pickles, please!
I have a tummy ache!

A Busy Guy

By Charnan Simon

Illustrated by Joan Holub

Daniel Robinson was a busy guy.

On Monday,
he planted a garden
for his mother . . .

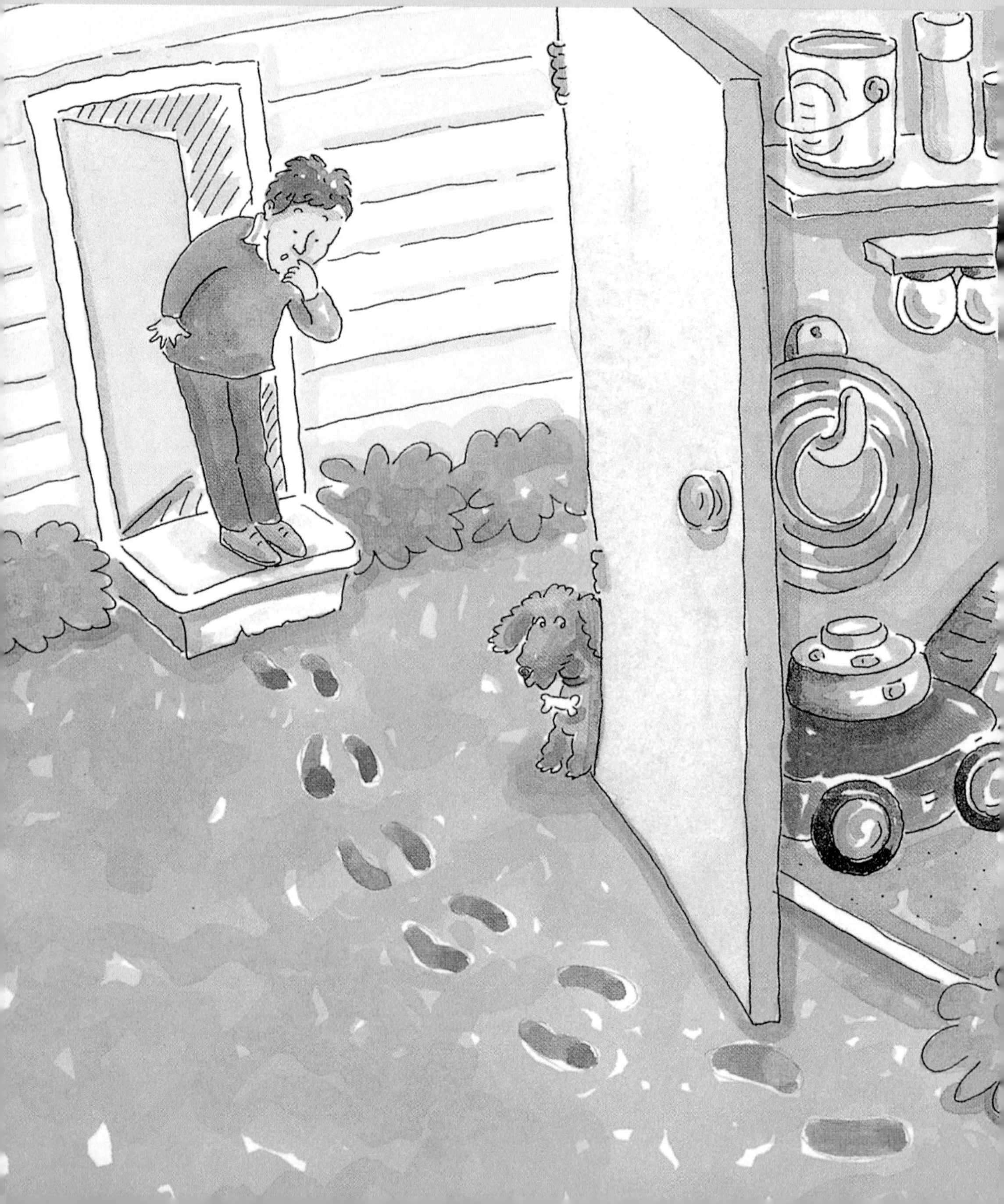

... and painted the toolshed for his father.

On Tuesday, he fixed up his bike;

then went to work on
his big sister's.

On Wednesday,
Daniel gave the dog
a haircut . . .

. . . and a bath.

On Thursday morning,
he operated on his little sister's
sick doll.

Thursday afternoon,
Daniel had to go shopping.

On Friday,
Daniel's friends came over to
build a fort . . .

. . . and fish in the creek.

On Saturday,
Daniel made breakfast for his
whole family,

then got to eat a
second breakfast at
the Pancake House.

On Sunday, Daniel rested.

Tomorrow would be another busy day.

Generous Me

By Mary E. Pearson

Illustrated by Gary Krejca

My sister whines and whines.
She says it isn't fair.

She tattles to my mom
that I refuse to share.

There are lots of things
that I would give her—all for free!
Things that she could *have*
if she wouldn't bother me!

I would give her my broccoli,

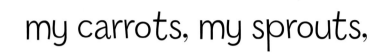

my carrots, my sprouts,

Mom's wet mushy kisses,

and all my time-outs.

The warts on my elbow,

my homework,

my chores,

and when I'm grounded,
the staying indoors.

My broken night-light,

the scab on my chin,

my wet slimy slugs
in their old rusty tin.

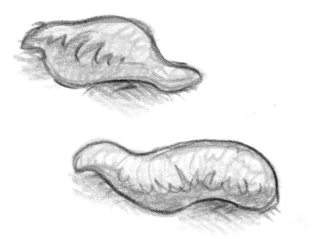

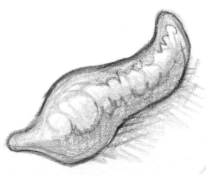

She says I won't share?
It just isn't true!

Why only last week,
I gave her the flu!

These pictures are all mixed up!

Tell what happened first, second, third, and last.

Tell about a time you learned to do something new.

Match the words that rhyme.

cake   eat
ice   ache
meat   slice

On Saturday, Daniel made breakfast.

What did he use to make breakfast?

What do you like to do on Saturdays?

A generous person is
someone who _____.

tattles   **shares**   **whines**

Tell about a time you were generous.

Library of Congress Cataloging-in-Publication Data

Wait, skates! and other funny stories.
    p. cm. -- (A Rookie reader treasury)
  Contents: Wait, skates! / by Mildred D. Johnson ; illustrated by Rick Stromoski -- Pickles in my soup / by Mary Pearson ;
illustrated by Tom Payne -- A busy guy / by Charnan Simon ; illustrated by Joan Holub -- Generous me / by Mary E. Pearson ;
illustrated by Gary Krejca

  ISBN-13: 978-0-531-20849-6
  ISBN-10: 0-531-20849-4
  1. Children's stories, American. 2. Humorous stories, American. [1. Humorous stories. 2. Short stories.] I. Title. II. Series.

  PZ5.W125 2009
  [E]--dc22

                        2008021945